# FESTINIOG
## 50 years of enterprise

Vic Mitchell

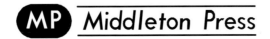
Middleton Press

*Cover picture:* **Blanche** *stands at Boston Lodge on 20th April 1986, the headboard commemorating 150 years of FR service. It never closed entirely. (J.Scrace)*

# This volume is dedicated to the staff and volunteers whose enterprise has made the railway a world leader, once again.

### Published on the 20th anniversary of the reopening of the FR to Blaenau Ffestiniog.

*Published  June 2002*

*ISBN  1 901706  83 4*

*© Middleton Press, 2002*

*Design        Deborah Esher*
*Typesetting   Barbara Mitchell*

*Published by*
*            Middleton Press*
*            Easebourne Lane*
*            Midhurst, West Sussex*
*            GU29 9AZ*
*Tel: 01730 813169*
*Fax: 01730 812601*

*Printed & bound by Biddles Ltd,*
*            Guildford and Kings Lynn*

# INDEX

# ACKNOWLEDGEMENTS

I am greatly appreciative of the assistance in checking the facts given by Allan Garraway, Jim Hewett and Arthur Lambert. As in previous albums, David and Susan Salter have ensured typographical accuracy and my wife, Barbara, has added her helpful ideas; thanks indeed.

I. Location map from 1982. (M.Seymour)

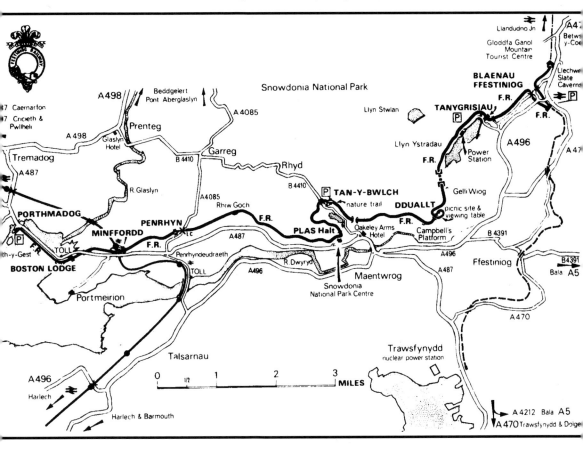

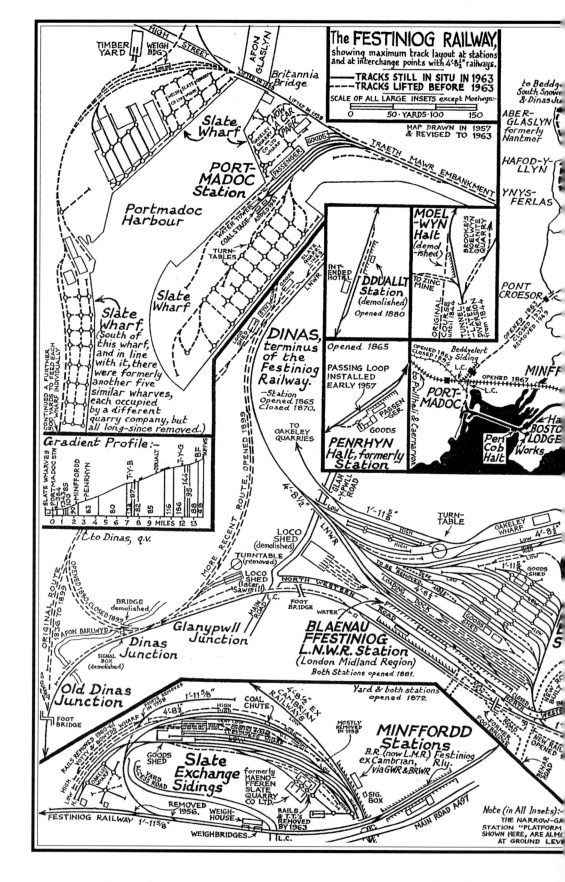

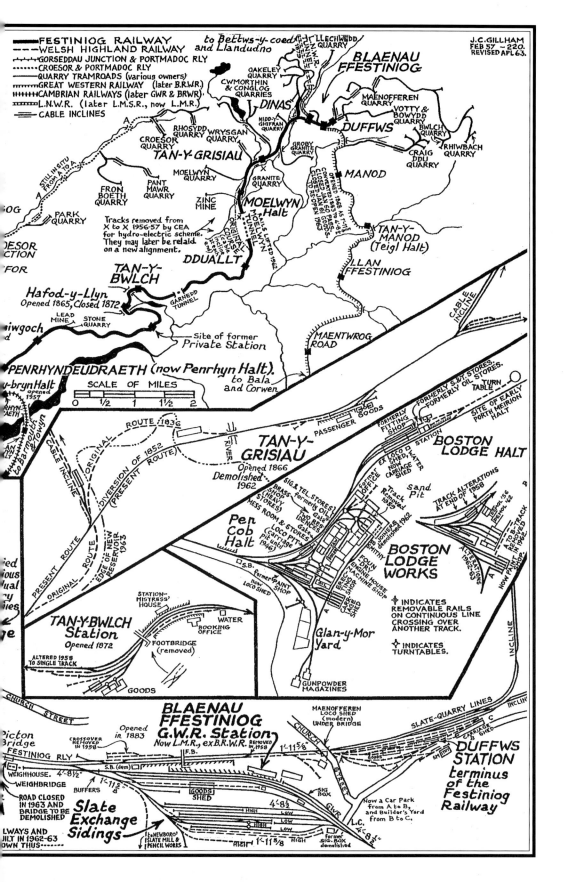

# PLACE NAMES

During the nineteenth century great efforts were made by outsiders to anglicise Wales, resulting in confusion in the spelling of place names. For historical accuracy and consistency, the form used by the railways in the period covered by this book is generally adopted.

The Festiniog Railway's Act of Parliament was passed with only one "F" and so the railway's name cannot easily be changed, although it is now marketed with two.

In giving a guide to pronunciation, it must be assumed that the reader has heard the unique Welsh sound of "ll". The places are listed in journey order.

| | |
|---|---|
| Minffordd | Mean-forth |
| Penrhyn | Pen-reen |
| Tan-y-bwlch | Tan-er-boolk |
| Dduallt | Thee-a*ll*t |

Portmadoc was renamed Porthmadog in 1974 despite having been built and named by Mr W.A.Madocks MP. The Welsh Prince Madog has gained fame for reputedly sailing to North America from a site north of the town, long before it existed. Both spellings are used in this album, depending on the period discussed.

Unfortunately, the three railways in Porthmadog are unhelpful to strangers by seldom making distinction between their stations, as was widely practised in the nineteenth century. Porthmadog North and Porthmadog Harbour would also be helpful to authors and their readers.

| | |
|---|---|
| Llyn Ystradau | *Ll*in erstradii |
| Tanygrisiau | Tan-er-grish-yah |
| Blaenau | Bly-nigh |

# PASSENGER SERVICES

The peak summer weekday timetables for the first years of FR extension are reproduced in our *Branch Lines around Porthmadog 1954-94*. Here we outline the development of services in respect of the number of trains that could be operated simultaneously on the line.

One train covered the timetables until 1958, when Tan-y-Bwlch was reached and an unadvertised afternoon relief train (known to the operators as "The Flying Flea") was run. The two trains met at the new terminus. This additional train departed at 3.0pm from Portmadoc and was advertised in the 1961 public timetable. From 1962, trains passed at Minffordd.

Extension to Dduallt in 1968 brought a three-train service for the first time, passing normally at Minffordd and Tan-y-Bwlch.

The provision of a loop at Rhiw Goch in 1975 allowed crossing of trains there each side of the summer peak weeks, when Minffordd and Tan-y-Bwlch were used. A fourth train set

(albeit third-class only) was introduced in 1977 for the peak service to Llyn Ystradau, this being the maximum number of trains to work at any one time. That year, a relief train at 17.00 from Porthmadog was worked on some days, bringing the number of departures to 15 in a day.

After the peak traffic years of the mid-1970s timetables were adjusted down to reflect demand. From May 1988, the peak service was hourly, all trains passing at Tan-y-Bwlch. There were ten departures from each terminus.

Short journeys have been operated on parts of the railway from time to time, notably Tan-y-Bwlch to Dduallt consequent upon reopening to the latter, and Dduallt northwards to allow passengers to view the recently-completed spiral line. Innovations in the 1990s included a Porthmadog-Minffordd shuttle service and a morning Blaenau Ffestiniog - Tan-y-Bwlch return journey.

# HISTORICAL BACKGROUND

An Act of Parliament was obtained in 1832 for the construction of the line, which was intended to facilitate the conveyance of slates from the quarries of the Blaenau Ffestiniog district to the shipping wharves at the then new town of Portmadoc. Gravity and horses were to be the main sources of motive power on the route, which was (six years after opening) on a continuous down gradient to the sea and nearly 14 miles in length.

Traffic commenced in 1836 and increased greatly, necessitating the replacement of the horses by steam locomotives in 1863 for hauling the empty slate wagons back to the quarries. Passenger traffic started officially in 1865.

The line prospered as a general carrier, double engines being introduced in 1869 to increase capacity. Blaenau Ffestiniog was reached by the London & North Western Railway in 1879 and by the Great Western Railway in 1882. By the end of the century, these factors, combined with a decreasing demand for slate, resulted in substantially reduced revenue for the FR.

The demands of World War I reduced the maintenance of the line and its ability to meet the competition of the emerging road transport industry after 1918. Despite the development of tourism between the wars and the hopes of expanding this traffic in association with the 1923 Welsh Highland Railway, the company's fortunes continued to decline.

World War II resulted in the cessation of passenger services on 15th September 1939 but slate trains continued until 1st August 1946.

A number of people made abortive attempts to revive the decaying railway but it was the enterprise of a young man, Leonard Heath Humphrys who called a meeting in Bristol in 1951, which led to the formation of the Festiniog Railway Society. Mr Alan Pegler succeeded in gaining control of the historic company on 24th June 1954 when new directors were appointed and the controlling interest was passed to a trust. Mr. Allan Garraway became manager in June 1955 and general manager from 1958 to 1983. With the support of a small staff and many FRS members, passenger services were re-started from Portmadoc as follows:

| To | Boston Lodge | 23 July 1955 |
|---|---|---|
| | Minffordd | 19 May 1956 |
| | Penrhyn | 20 April 1957 |
| | Tan-y-bwlch | 5 April 1958 |
| | Dduallt | 6 April 1968 |
| | Llyn Ystradau | 25 June 1977 |
| | Tanygrisiau | 24 June 1978 |
| | Blaenau Ffestiniog | 25 May 1982 |

# GEOGRAPHICAL SETTING

Portmadoc and its harbour were established in the 1820s, as the construction of the embankment or Cob resulted in the Afon Glaslyn scouring a deep channel near the tidal sluices. The port was suitable for the ships of the period and the town expanded as a result of the increasing trade, being laid out in a grid-iron pattern, as was common in new towns of industrial Britain.

The FR terminus is at the Harbour and its first mile traverses the level Cob. Thereafter the line was on a continuous rising gradient. To Penrhyndeudraeth the route is along a tapering finger of high ground that separates the valleys of the Glaslyn and the Dwyryd, the latter river being the main feature of the Vale of Ffestiniog. By Dduallt, the line is over 500ft above the valley floor and passes through part of the Moelwyn mountain range by means of a tunnel. In this vicinity granite was of economic importance, but the predominant mineral worked from here northwards is slate of high quality.

From Tanygrisiau the route runs up the valley of the Afon Barlwyd. It is in the urban area of Blaenau Ffestiniog for its final mile, being overshadowed by mountains and slate rubbish tips. The town is one of the highest in Wales at over 700ft above sea level.

# INTRODUCTION

Those intent on reviving the railway were motivated by its historical significance in world railway history. However, anyone passing by in the closure period would have simply regarded it as a linear nature reserve and/or scrap yard, as shown in some of the illustrations herein.

The success of steam on such a narrow gauge had confounded the critics, such as the widely respected Robert Stephenson (of *Rocket* fame) but in 1870 the Imperial Russian Commission arrived on the line to witness the astonishing performance of a double engine, built to Robert Fairlie's patented design. Delegations from other parts of the world followed and the Festiniog principle spread internationally.

Not only was the FR a pioneer with narrow gauge steam traction, but it used the first bogie coach built for service in Great Britain. It also instigated extensive technical innovation in many other fields.

The initiative and enterprise shown by a large number of persistent individuals in the early 1950s is outlined in the diagram opposite. It was drawn in 1979 by Dan Wilson, but has since been found to contain a few minor flaws. However, it does convey the extent of the effort made by so many to restore this badly tarnished jewel in the crown of railway history, which forms part of the industrial heritage of the United Kingdom.

Once announced, the Society grew at a very healthy rate and local groups were formed in Birmingham and London in 1955. Others soon followed and in 2001 they comprised Bristol, Dee & Mersey, East Anglian, East Midlands, Gloucestershire, Hants & Sussex, Lancashire & Cheshire, London, Midland, Milton Keynes, North Staffs, Northumbria, Sheffield & District, Upper Thames and White Rose. In addition, there was the all important Heritage Group, to care for matters historical. Within these organisations there are deep wells of enterprise to be drawn upon for the continuing benefit of the FR.

The prolonged legal battle to obtain compensation for the cost of reinstatement of the line submerged under a lake forming the lower part of a pumped storage hydro-electric system brought forth further examples of individual enterprise. Tenacity was another attribute, as the case took 16 years to complete, a record time.

A new alignment was required which necessitated the construction of a fresh tunnel and the country's only spiral line. Known as The Deviation, this major civil engineering project attracted a new brand of volunteer and much of the work was undertaken in the traditional laborious manner. Again, the FR was involved with an enterprise unparalleled in world railway history.

Fresh initiatives were made to complete the remainder of the route and to create a new terminus jointly with BR at Blaenau Ffestiniog. The outstanding success of the FR revival had earlier inspired a group of French railway enthusiasts to emulate it and the equally scenic Chemin de Fer du Vivarais was saved from extinction. It is twinned with the FR.

This album generally features the practical illustrations of enterprise, but there have been (and hopefully will continue to be) many examples of successful administrative initiatives. These range from the establishment of a worldwide travel business to major fund raising galas and other enthusiast events, together with the publication of guide books, films, magazines and so on.

There have inevitably been differences of opinion between managers and the managed. One of the former once reminded staff that the projects were all "Jolly Good Fun". Works rolling stock numbers were soon prefixed with JGF and subsequently this annotation unwittingly appeared in a railway stock book.

I hope that those who have left the railway recently for various reasons will be encouraged by the photographs that follow to realise that it is a continued healthy future for the FR that is our prime concern. Hopefully this volume might inspire them to return with their own brand of enterprise.

I include a number of photographs of the closure period to illustrate the starting point. Significantly the revival took place aptly in an uphill direction, as it has been an uphill struggle! My involvement as a founder, early FRS director and occasional volunteer enables me to salute all those who have applied their enterprise more intimately to this exceptional railway over the last 50 years. I make no apology for the repeated use of the word "enterprise" herein.

*Midhurst 2002*                    *Vic Mitchell*

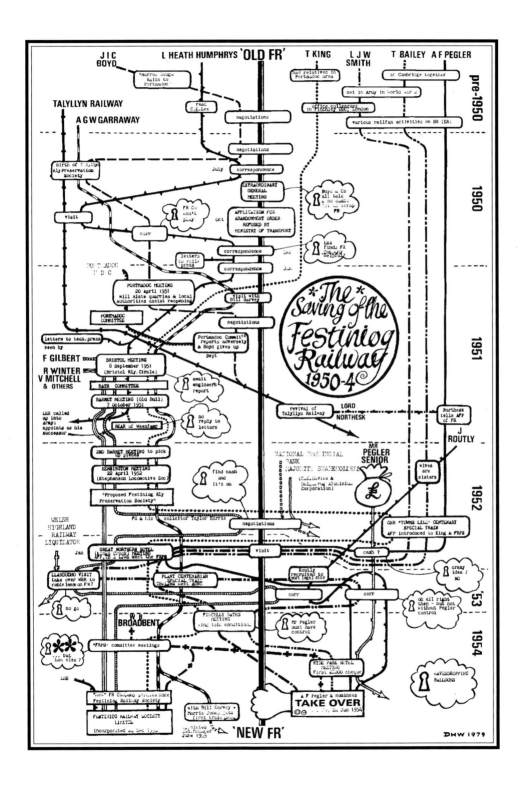

*The Saving of the Festiniog Railway 1950-4*

# PUBLICATIONS

The FR could probably claim more column inches per mile than any other railway in the world, the figure being particularly high in the last 50 years. The first major work in that period was J.I.C.Boyd's history, which is still the standard reference source. Many books have subsequently come and gone.

The FRS initially had a newsletter, which was upgraded to the FR Magazine in 1958 and has been published quarterly ever since. The groups have also produced their own commendable communications.

Enterprising members of the Heritage Group have published the 278 page *FR Chronology - New Millenium Edition*. Sadly its last entry records the death of Leonard Heath Humphrys, founder of the FRS, nine days before the end of the century. A few extracts from this edition are reproduced herein, the Magazine references being year/month/day, volume-page. This is an essential aid to students of recent FR history; also included therein are many pages of pre-1950 data.

All current books on the FR and its environs are available from the FR shop in Harbour Station, Porthmadog, LL49 9NF.

1. The directors of the newly formed FRS Ltd decided to show some models at the annual Model Railway Club's exhibition in London to launch the revival scheme publicly. I suggested that press reporters were more interested in models of the female type and volunteered my fiancee to pose as the once-famous FR station mistress. Barbara is seen on 12th April 1955, following an embarrassing interview with a Welsh journalist. Her boss thought that she was absent for a dental appointment; it was partially true as I was a student at Guy's Hospital Dental School at that time. (V.Mitchell)

The traffic figures appear to show history repeating itself, with the WHR having an adverse effect on the FR. The FR took a lease in 1934 on the WHR, which had been bankrupt since 1927. The venture continued to run at a loss and was closed at the end of 1936. When attempting to relinquish the lease, the FR stated "that the WHR does not appeal to the public in anything like the same degree as does our own railway". (The reasons are given on page V of *Branch Lines around Portmadoc 1923-46*). The graph, which was produced by Graham Ive, shows the extent of the FR's second involvement, but this time as owner. The mileage is due to increase greatly.

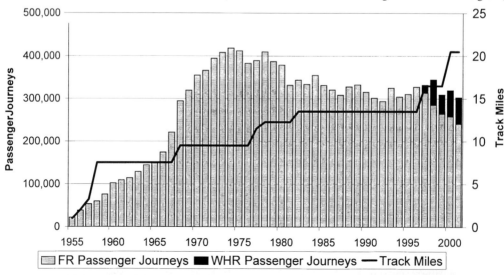

# PORTMADOC

2.　　　Two photographs from the early 1950s show that the FR presented the worst possible image to those interested in it by storing abandoned stock at its principle station. The advent of World War II precluded the consideration of such matters and there were few other places available for storage. The railway was effectively closed below Minffordd after 1939, except for loco movements to Boston Lodge. (J.H.Meredith)

3.　　　On the extreme left of the previous picture is this historic turtle-roofed van, so described by Victorian coach builders. Numbered 3, it was almost at the point of collapse. Fifty years later, plans were being made to create a replica.　(D.Rendell/M.Davies)

4.    The first train movement under the new management took place on 21st September 1954 and two days later the Simplex and no. 10 were recorded with the forthcoming manager at the controls and the outgoing manager on the right. Robert Evans had worked for the FR for 60 years. (A.G.W.Garraway)

5.    The clearance of the station environs was well advanced when the Simplex was photographed again. The date was 7th November 1954 and the end of the "platform" is in the foreground. (A.G.W.Garraway)

6.    The reopening took place at short notice on 23rd July 1955, approval to operate at 10mph having been given only two days earlier. Mainly locals witnessed the official reopening ceremony of the 28th; the line was now under the control of "English eccentrics". Sadly relatively few Welsh people became involved in reviving this piece of their national heritage; there is still the opportunity to help to enhance it! (A.G.W.Garraway)

7.      Initially the one-mile service was operated by coaches 23 and 12, hauled by the Simplex which had been intended for short-term use in World War I. Its magneto proved unsuited to the new demands made on it, being in need of an overhaul. My Barbara, seen in picture no. 1, had her first encounter with the FR on 30th July 1955 and her tasks have subsequently ranged from buffet car operation to production of this text. (V.Mitchell)

⎯⎯⎯⎯⎯▶

8.      Built in 1863, *Prince* was photographed on 2nd August 1955 at the start of its new life of service to the FR. The engine had been stripped and was under overhaul during the War, with a new boiler delivered not long before operation of the railway ceased. The Company did try to sell it, but of course if was no use to anyone else. It was claimed to be the oldest regularly used locomotive in the world. (A.G.W.Garraway)

⎯⎯⎯⎯⎯▶

9.      *Prince* operated most of the trains in that first short season, which ended on 24th September and recorded about 20,000 passenger journeys. The return fare across The Cob for adults was one shilling. Slates were still missing from the goods shed as *Prince* returns with one of the last trains of 1955. (A.M.Davies)

10.     April 1956 was the time for a major effort by volunteers to improve the diabolical trackwork at the approach to the station. Previously there had been only emergency spot resleepering at the joints on the Cob. Secondhand BR sleepers, cut in half, were used until 1970, since when new jarrah ones from Australia have been used. (A.G.W.Garraway)

11.    The former connection with the Welsh Highland Railway next to the goods shed was a convenient place to unload potentially useful stock. A Scammell reverses in on 26th August 1957 with a Peckett 0-6-0ST from Harrogate Gasworks. It required modification to make it suitable for the FR, and was eventually sold in 1987 - see *Kent Narrow Gauge* picture no. 67 to find it in rebuilt form. (A.G.W.Garraway)

12.    By the Summer of 1958, the FR was being overwhelmed by passengers and the enterprising management assembled a relief train comprised of some of the original four-wheeled coaches. "The Flying Flea" is being prepared for its first run (to Penrhyn only) on 4th August 1958. It left at 2.45pm for Tan-y-Bwlch on most weekdays for the rest of that month. (A.G.W.Garraway)

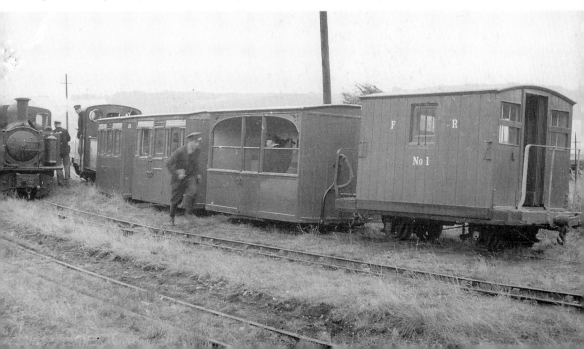

13.　　More unusual activity was recorded near the goods shed, this time on 30th May 1959 when new tanks for the Fairlie *Merddin Emrys* arrived on a member's lorry. After much effort, the locomotive was put into steam on 21st April 1961. (A.G.W.Garraway)

14.　　The box seen against the sky is a TV camera; it is mounted on a wagon ready for a live broadcast on 13th July 1960 and its power leads run back along coach 22 to a mobile generator on another wagon. This piece of enterprise resulted in many additional passengers, none of whom fell into the inspection pit fortunately. (A.G.W.Garraway)

15.　　Track realignment and removal of the unusual stub points (near the water tank) was undertaken in March 1964 in connection with the development of South Snowdon Wharf for residential purposes. The level crossing (right) was being eliminated. (A.G.W.Garraway)

16. *Princess* was the first to steam on the old FR (on 28th July 1863) and the last (on 1st August 1946). It is seen on display on 26th June 1964 and has served the railway in this manner ever since; in Blaenau Ffestiniog from 1969, at the Stockton & Darlington Railway celebrations in 1975 and in the FR Museum since 1981. (J.H.Meredith)

————————▶

17. Built by the American Locomotive Company (Alco) in 1917 for use in World War I, this fine 2-6-2T remained in use in France until 1964. It was purchased by enterprising member John Ransom and donated to the FR, where it is seen on 18th October 1967 soon after its arrival. It was named *Mountaineer* in 1968 and its appearance drastically altered subsequently. (A.G.W.Garraway)

————————▶

18. This is "Blockade Sunday" when stock, including *Palmerston*, was parked here on 3rd December 1967. The locomotive was still nominally pink, following a prank in 1965. It was sold in 1974. Last run in 1940, it was returned to steam in 1993 and used on special occasions only. (A.G.W.Garraway)

19.    A special type of enterprise is required to keep the FR's fleet of diesel locomotives on the road. Seldom photographed, the driving wheels of *Upnor Castle* were outside the goods shed on 17th February 1968. Requiring even more specialised skills is the ballast tamper, seen in the background prior to unloading. It had to be converted from standard gauge.
(A.G.W.Garraway)

→

20.    A locomotive crisis developed in the early 1960s and the enterprising management took the opportunity of acquiring two Hunslet-built locomotives from the Penrhyn Quarry, where they had been used on its main line. The 0-4-0ST *Blanche* is seen on 26th May 1968; she became a 2-4-0ST in February 1972, having been given a new tender with a cab, in 1965.
(J.H.Meredith)

→

21.    "Portmadoc" was changed to "Porthmadog" in 1974 and the buildings were drastically altered that year. Seen in March is the steelwork that would create a buffet on the ground floor and more office space above. The archives would be located in the goods shed loft. (A.G.W.Garraway)

22.    The FR's Jones crane was employed to raise the frame members for the base of a new water tank in March 1974. The railway had unfortunately become squeezed between new dwellings and their access road. The view from the station, one of the top tourist locations, was ruined by the "planners" for ever. (A.G.W.Garraway)

23.    *Prince* was recorded on 26th May 1980, waiting to depart for Tanygrisiau at 10.10. The control office for the railway is above the cab. A canopy for the platform did not arrive until 1987, 122 years later and a welcome addtion. The delay was due to lack of funds, not lack of enterprise. The name of the buffet was changed from *Little Wonder* to *Spooner's* in 1999, it subsequently remaining open all evening. (J.Scrace)

24.     There have been many high profile events at the station, but the quiet reintroduction of coach 15 to traffic on 21st August 2001 was not one of them. The running gear was built at Boston Lodge in 1872 and the body by Brown Marshalls & Company. It was the first bogie coach to run in Britain and it was restored to three-class configuration with the help of the Heritage Lottery Fund. (V.Mitchell)

THE COB

← ———— 25. Harbour Station is in the background as we start our journey up the line and back in time. Seen in June 1957, the signal post, which had come from Blaenau in 1927, lasted until 1967, when it fell down in a gale. (D.Clayton)

26. Boston Lodge Works and the former quarry in which it was built is in the background of this photograph from 26th May 1968. No. 3 *Earl of Merioneth* had been *Taliesin* until 1961; it had been returned to service after much effort in 1957. (J.H.Meredith)

27. Low sun and mist on a calm morning created a pleasant ambience in which to admire the achievements of the permanent way personnel on 5th May 2001. Between the tracks is a modern flashing light to draw attention to the catch point, while an historic disc signal serves as a STOP sign. (V.Mitchell)

# BOSTON LODGE
# WORKS

28.    The works is in the background of this photograph from July 1950 featuring the quietly rotting stock. The vehicles with the hoops were "tourist cars"; sadly they had no future, but a replica was built in 1971. Living in retirement in one of the nearby railway cottages was The Revd. Timmy Phillips. Enterprisingly, he established an honorary one-man security service, keeping doors and windows secure. (J.H.Meredith)

---

**Boston Lodge,** 56/06/01,N07-3, Large number of broken windows have been replaced and much of the roof of the carriage shed (the old paint shop in the west yard) has been re-slated.

**Boston Lodge,** 56/09/01,N08-2, The new locomotive pit in the erecting shop has been completed and handed over to the locomotive department for use.

29.     From front to back in this May 1952 view is the hydraulic test pump, one of the bogies from *Taliesin*, the then petrol driven Simplex and an abandoned Morris 8. The enterprising resuscitators had to first install electricity in order to work efficiently and at night. The latter was often necessary to maintain the service.  (A.G.W.Garraway)

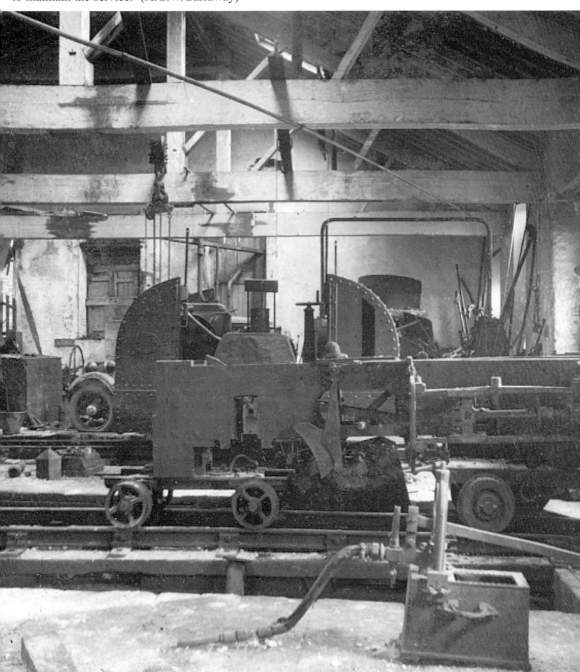

30. The erecting shop was soon rendered usable, but this August 1956 panorama shows that one of its windows was still covered with a corrugated iron sheet. Also included is the long shed in which a wheel drop was later installed. Nearby is the Baldwin "tractor". (A.G.W.Garraway)

31.     The gate post had become slightly deformed and attempts to remedy it with a chain attached to the Baldwin in January 1957 ended in a total disaster. Named *Moelwyn* that month, it had been built in the USA in 1918 with a petrol engine. The 0-4-0 was fitted with a diesel engine and converted to a 2-4-0 later in 1957. Prior to that it could be turned on a wagon turntable, hence its rotation since the previous picture. (A.G.W.Garraway)

**Boston Lodge,** 56/09/01,20-15,  Glan-y-mor carriage shed (and roof) had been badly damaged at sometime during the closed years by a boulder having fallen from the quarry face above.

**Boston Lodge,** 56/09/01,N08-3, The roof of Glan-y-mor carriage shed has been propped up to permit release of carriages 18 and 20; the collapsed roof proved difficult to demolish completely in spite of its precarious condition; the Simplex was used to drag it down in pieces until demolition was complete.

32.    Described in caption 24, no. 15 was rather poorly in June 1958, but its historic significance was recognised. Considerable enterprise was required for its restoration and it returned to traffic on 9th August 1960, albeit with only half the compartments in use. Evening and weekend work meant that it was complete by the end of the month. (A.G.W.Garraway)

33.    We saw the top bogie for *Taliesin* in picture 29; this is its bottom one undergoing valve setting on 30th December 1958. The designation refers to the top and bottom of the railway. The ball of the flexible steam joint is evident, a detail seldom on view. (A.G.W.Garraway)

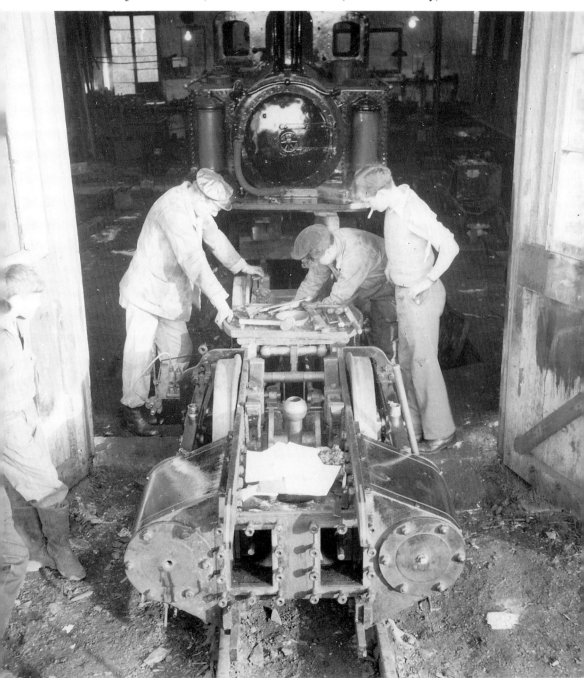

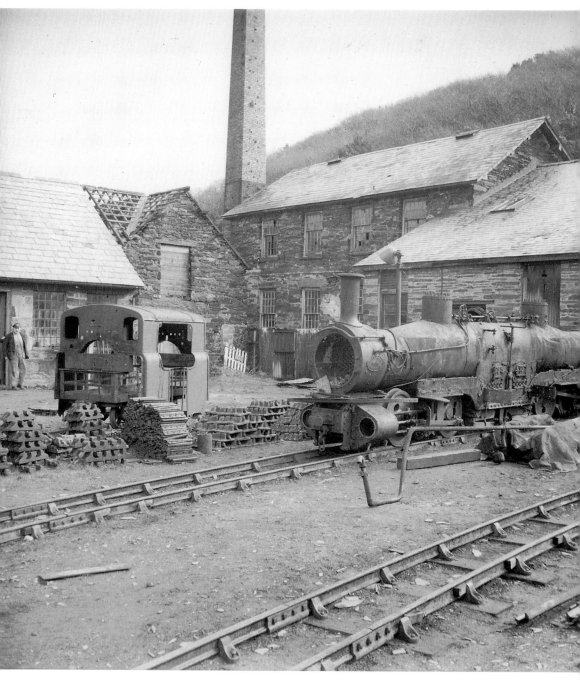

34.     The massive task of restoring *Merddin Emrys* had progressed thus far by May 1959, but its first steaming did not take place until 21st April 1961, due to the demands of the elderly operating locomotives. New cradles, smokeboxes and tanks were made for it and the inevitable retubing took place. It ran without a cab for a long time, as the original was too rotten to replace. (A.G.W.Garraway)

35.     The coaching crisis resulted in some enterprising folk recovering a chicken house from the site of the Lynton & Barnstaple Railway in Devon. It had to be dismantled and rebuilt to the FR's smaller profile. *Moelwyn* is about to check clearances on 14th May 1959, so that reassembly could start. It was fittted with a kitchen and was completed in 1963, when it was numbered 14. Hens were also evicted from a former WHR coach which now runs on the FR as no. 26. (A.G.W.Garraway)

36.     *Blanche* was the second PQR locomotive to arrive and is seen on The Cob on 17th December 1963, prior to unloading at Boston Lodge Halt. On the skyline on that dull day are the remains of the works gateway and the pre-1923 signal box. The arch on the left had once served as a road entrance to the works. (A.G.W.Garraway)

37.　　Taken to show the problem of the removal of a "monolith" from the works floor in August 1962, the photograph includes some of the Victorian line shafting and flat belts used for conveying power to machine tools. They had once been powered by a stationary engine, this using steam from *Palmerston's* boiler. The management later installed a Crossley hot bulb diesel engine. (A.G.W.Garraway)

38.    Looking in the opposite direction to that of picture no. 31, we witness track improvements in May 1963. The building on the left was used as a running shed, whereas the old FR used one on the opposite side of the main line. The wood on the right was used for fire lighting. (A.G.W.Garraway)

39.    In the foreground in this March 1964 panorama is Glan-y-Mor Yard, then used for a dumping ground for inoperable stock. The crane is in the centre and is being used to assist in the erection of a carriage shed. The Royal Engineers were involved in this task. Another and larger shed was started in 1974. (A.G.W.Garraway)

40.     The Long Shed is seen again in this photograph from February 1965, which features the new bogie design for future coaches. That year was the centenary of FR passenger service and initially the new profile vehicles were known as "Centenary Stock" and numbered from 100. The unflattering term of "Barns" was used later; "Cents" might be better. (A.G.W.Garraway)

**Coach No. 100,** 65/01/01,28-7,  Virtually complete structurally and fitting out proceeds steadily, work being done entirely by Fred Boughey and his gang.

**Coach No. 100,** 65/05/24,29-4,  New Observation Car launched on 24th May 1965 and entered traffic next day.

41.    The yard tidiness had improved greatly by May 1968 when *Moelwyn* was photographed between the breakdown van and a coal wagon. The dirty and laborious task of coaling ended as a regular chore in October 1972, after which time most of the fleet burnt oil. The old foundry chimney lasted until 1978. (J.H.Meredith)

**Boston Lodge,** 67/02/14,36-5, New lathe has at last arrived and being installed in machine shop. Part of blacksmith's shop made over to S&T Dept. as point fitters' workshop and store.

**Boston Lodge,** 67/08/15,38-4, New shed in Glan-y-mor has been roofed, doors being fitted. Work started on extension of long road of loco. shed into it.

42.　　The new cab profile for *Mountaineer* can be compared with the original seen in picture 17. The unusual posture for travel had been adopted by Mary Stevenson who was making a promotional film called "Festiniog Country". (A.G.W.Garraway)

43.　　Seen in July 1973 is the framework for a new fabrication shop, by far the largest structural enterprise to have been undertaken by the new management. It was built behind the erecting shop, as an extension to it. Sadly, most of the coaches still had to stand in the open. (A.G.W.Garraway)

44.　　The *Earl of Merioneth* had its top bogie stripped in August 1974. Eventually all such power bogies were standardised so that they were interchangeable. Thus when one locomotive was having prolonged boiler repairs, these most expensive parts could earn revenue under another machine. (A.G.W.Garraway)

45.    A very notable enterprise was the construction of the single Fairlie *Taliesin* in the works in 1995-99. It was similar to one completed in the same premises in 1876, but dismantled in 1932. It was also named *Taliesin*, a name carried by the *Earl of Merioneth* from 1956-1961. It was photographed on 15th May 1999; it entered public service on 28th August of that year. (V.Mitchell)

——————→

46.    With the destruction of the Long Shed in 1988 and the loss of the south wall, this view of the old erecting shop was possible on 30th April 2000. On the right is another example of Boston Lodge enterprise. Completed there in 1992 is double Fairlie *David Lloyd George*, carrying a comic face. Behind it is *Vale of Ffestiniog*, a diesel built in South Africa by Funkey in 1967, delivered to the FR in 1993 and reduced in dimensions to enter traffic in 1998. (V.Mitchell)

——————→

47.    The steelwork for the Glan-y-Mor carriage shed (left) was completed early in 1991 and low level floors were provided therein for easy bogie servicing. To the right of it in this April 2000 photograph is the lottery-funded Heritage Centre erected for the maintenance and restoration of historic rolling stock and officially opened on 7th October 1999. We are looking at the back of it, towards the main line. (V.Mitchell)

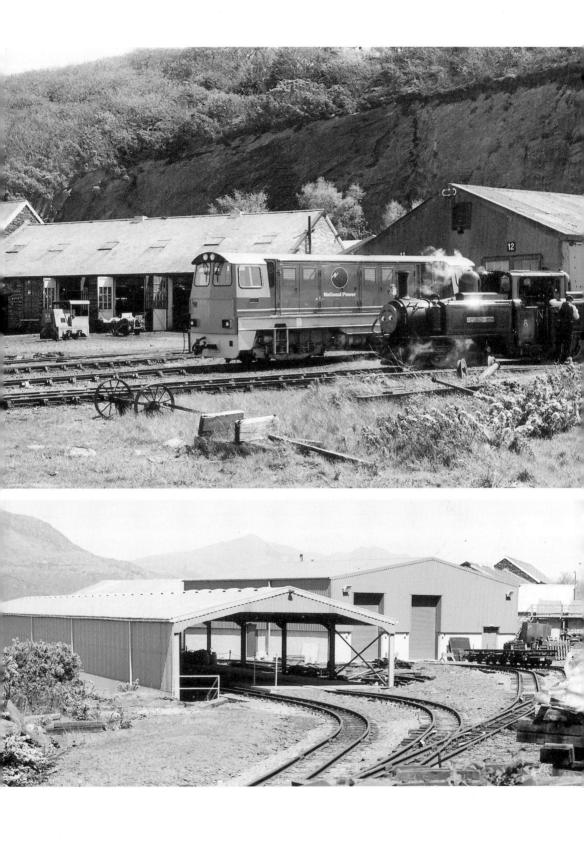

———————▶

48.　　Coach 15, seen in picture 24, was the first to benefit from the Heritage Centre and its repairs were similarly funded. The scheme also included renovation work on the fleet of slate wagons, some of which are unique and from different sources. This view is at about 90 degrees to the previous one. (V.Mitchell)

49.　　Moving to the upper yard in 2000, we see the then new road access (right) and the old one (left). In the centre is the former locomotive superintendents office and the main line is to the left of it, as is the siding leading to the subject of the next picture. Sadly the world's oldest railway works is now infested with motor cars, even on special occasions when a car free zone would be appropriate and appreciated. (V.Mitchell)

———————▶

50.　　Boston Lodge Halt is in the distance in this view of the former running shed, which was used as such until 1946. It had been used for coach storage in the revival era, but it is seen on 26th June 1994 serving its original function in a re-enactment exactly 40 years after the takeover. On the left is *Prince* and on the right is the coal-fired *Palmerston*. (V.Mitchell)

51.    The bridge carrying the main road over the FR was replaced during the Winter of 1959-60 in connection with road improvements; the temporary level crossing is visible in the distance. The new one was built with greater clearance, which allowed the building of the larger coaches mentioned in caption 40. The surplus material from this work was taken to Tan-y-Bwlch for embankment strengthening. (N.F.Gurley)

52.    The embankment below the bridge failed due to a blocked culvert in March 1981 , leaving the track unsupported and the railings deformed. The scene was recorded in rain on the 11th. The slip had been due to flood water above the line washing away sand on which the bank had been founded. It was a particularly inconvenient time, as all effort was being directed towards the completion of the line. (A.G.W.Garraway)

# SOUTH OF MINFFORDD

53.    Work was undertaken in January 1957 to improve the clearance at Quarry Lane crossing where the FR had a cottage for the crossing keeper. Until a width restriction was placed on the highway, tipper lorries squeezed between the stone gate posts many times each day. It had for long been known as Lottie's Crossing, after its popular one-time resident keeper. (A.G.W.Garraway)

54.    The projecting stonework over the front door is clearer in this photograph from August 2001, as is the steepness of the lane. The automatic flashing lights came into use on 28th October 1991 and the cottage continues to be occupied by FR staff. (V.Mitchell)

**Minffordd,** 56/09/01, N08-2, The derelict hut at Minffordd Station, reputed once to have been the old station at Hafod-y-Llyn, has been demolished and the remnants stacked in the works yard for firewood.

**Minffordd,** 56/09/01, N08-3, The two cross-overs opposite the Minffordd weigh-house have been removed

**Minffordd,** 57/01/01, N09-4, A new gate has been made for Minffordd level crossing from the roof off Glan-y-mor carriage shed. The massive stone gateposts have now been lifted out and re-erected in new positions to meet Ministry of Transport requirements.

# MINFFORDD

55.    The quarry is in the background of this 1958 panorama from the bridge that carries the FR over the Cambrian Coast line. Slate was still stored on the wharves and coal, ballast and other materials for the FR came into the sidings in the centre of the picture. The last consignment to arrive by BR was rail from Tilbury on 30th May 1972. The slate sheds were adapted for carriage storage in 1970. (J.H.Meredith)

56.    *Linda* arrived by rail on 14th July 1962 and is seen being shunted the next day. The 0-4-0 became a 2-4-0 in 1969. She is adjacent to the former goods transfer shed, which was leased out to a timber merchant until 1964. Thereafter it was used by the permanent way staff. Initially, *Linda* was on hire. (A.G.W.Garraway)

57.    Parts of the footbridge at Blaena, South Wales, arrived by rail in January 1969. It was intended for bridge replacement at the top end of the line at a later date. A very wide range of ex-BR material found its way to the FR. (A.G.W.Garraway)

58. A close-up of the FR's Jones crane in May 1973 includes a rail stockpile in the background. The vehicle had limitations owing to the geography of the line. The first dwelling that my wife and I had is on the left. After we acquired a fixed abode in 1960, we moved it here and it was used by other members of the Hants & Sussex Group before going to Boston Lodge Top Yard. (A.G.W.Garraway)

59. Despite working long and hard in Boston Lodge, a group of five folk had sufficient energy and enterprise left to purchase the 1899 Hunslet *Britomart* in 1965 and to restore it to working order. Stored in the works, it only appears occasionally in public, such as the FR 150 event. It is seen on 20th April 1986 in the company of visiting 0-4-0VB *Chaloner* prior to a slate wagon gravity run from nearby Gwindy Bank. (J.Scrace)

60. Standing in the sidings between the main line (foreground) and the rail storage area is the Permanent Way Department's train. This enterprising group created this vast improvement on the lineside hut. It comprises a mess coach, with catering and toilet facilities, and a tool wagon, with two stores and a generator. This and the next two pictures were taken in August 2001. (V.Mitchell)

61.    The exterior is shown as a reminder that the Buildings, Parks & Gardens Department (established 1992) has maintenance tasks beyond that seen from the train. Also included is *Blanche* running over the bottom loop points and an old building (right) believed to have been stables in the pre-steam days. (V.Mitchell)

62.    A remarkable enterprise was the creation of a replica of the waiting shelter that had stood on the down platform until May 1956. It was a joint venture by the Heritage and London Area Groups; it had been subject to a trial assembly in a suburban garden, no doubt to the dismay of the neighbours. An even greater enterprise can be seen in the background - it is the 1995 Volunteers Hostel and Training Centre. (V.Mitchell)

**PENRHYN**

63.     A 1952 view reveals that part of the FR property had been adopted as a thoroughfare by local residents. However, the rails were still present below the undergrowth on the right. (D.Rendell)

64.     Taken in the oppposite direction from almost the same viewpoint, we witness clearance work in October 1956. The level crossing gates and the keepers hut are visible. These gates were still manually operated almost 50 years later and volunteer operatives are usually being sought. (A.G.W.Garraway)

65.    Another photograph from the same day shows wagons being manhandled into the solitary siding, last used to bring flour to the adjacent bakery. The Baldwin would soon be released so that it could propel the wagons up to the clearance site. (A.G.W.Garraway)

66.    A loop was laid so that the station could serve as a terminus in the 1957 season; *Taliesin* was recorded on a trial run on 24th March. The buildings were used as a store for many years and were adapted to serve as a volunteers hostel in 1971. (A.G.W.Garraway)

67.    *Prince* is ready to return to Portmadoc in June 1957 and to pass over the crossing seen in picture 65. The loop was used for passing trains from 1961, but their increasing length necessitated the provision of a headshunt in 1969. A Saturdays-only service for shoppers was run to the end of 1957, the enterprise being inadequately supported. (D.Clayton)

68.    A successful "1920s Weekend" was staged on 5th-6th June 1993, one of the highlights being a gravity slate train although it ran in low light in the early evening. The train is running towards us and is approaching the station. (V.Mitchell)

69.     After 1973 trains could pass at Minffordd, Tan-y-Bwlch and Dduallt. To improve operating flexibility a loop was created at Rhiw Goch. It is seen in August 1974, as signalling work was beginning. A nine-lever signal box was ready for the 1975 peak season. (A.G.W.Garraway)

# TAN-Y-BWLCH

70.　A 1952 view shows the original station building. The house, hidden on the left, was occupied by Will Jones and his wife, both former FR employees. Will had worked on the track and so cared for the railway that he continued to oil the points here during the closure period. He returned to his former post after the reopening and passed his knowledge on to many. (D.Rendell)

71.　The line below the station became impassible, even on foot. The track had been cleared of saplings and other undergrowth by the time that this photograph was taken on 5th December 1954. The Simplex was not supposed to be producing steam, but such was the problem with its fan belt. (A.G.W.Garraway)

72.　Caught on film outside the house at the still-closed station on 12th November 1956 was Bessie Jones. She had gained fame before the war as the stationmistress in Welsh national costume, referred to in caption 1. Her enterprise involved the sale of teas and postcards. The couple retired in 1968. (A.G.W.Garraway)

73.    The area was tidied before passenger trains returned in 1958, but much grass remained to add to the rural charm. The sign in front of the Mini announces TEAS AT STATION HOUSE. The locomotive is *Earl of Merioneth*, one of the titles of HRH Prince Philip, and was recorded on 14th July 1962. (J.Scrace)

74.    A panorama from 26th May 1968 shows the tender cab of *Blanche* clearly and also new track in the foreground. This was part of a fresh alignment that would very soon allow construction of an island platform. The old buildings were saved from demolition and restored. (J.H.Meredith)

75.     The footbridge had progressed thus far by February 1971 and fencing had been provided by the North Staffs Group. In the background is the former goods shed on which work started in 1968 to convert it to a cafe and shop. A toilet block was added behind it, in favour of the provisions in the old station. The bridge came into use on 18th July 1971. (A.G.W.Garraway)

76.     As part of the events to mark the 40th anniversary of the takeover, a freight train was operated on 26th June 1994, hauled by *Prince*. The signal box (left) was fitted with a lever frame in 1972, but it was never used, hence the levers on the left for the siding. Instead, the loop points were fitted with electric motors, worked from the relay room. (J.Scrace)

# DDUALLT

77.　The south end of Moelwyn Tunnel was photographed on 15th July 1951, three weeks after your scribe had stumbled through it without a torch. Not only were many sleepers under water, but there were invisible voids between them. To add to the difficulties, there were rotting sheep carcases at each end. (A.G.W.Garraway)

78.　This is the view in the opposite direction, but on 22nd September 1957, when *Prince* ventured over the decrepit track thus far, with coach no. 10. There had been 15 trips through the tunnel between January 1955 and January 1957, mainly to recover materials and wagons. One journey was to meet Central Electricity Authority representatives who thought that the line was completely impassible! (A.G.W.Garraway)

79.　Linda was recorded with a ballast train on the newly laid track on 3rd November 1967. By that time new stone was obtained from the quarry seen in the background of Minffordd picture nos. 54 and 55. Spent ballast from BR had been used until earlier that year. (A.G.W.Garraway)

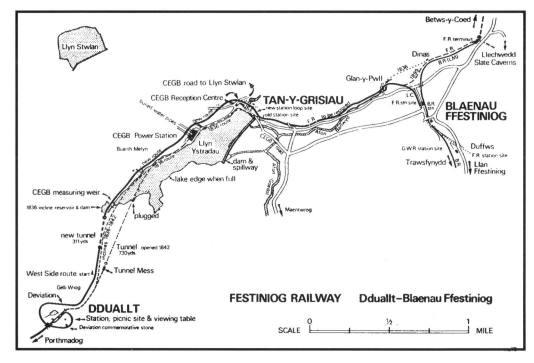

III. This 1973 map indicates the alignment and lengths of the new and old tunnels, together with the position of the incline that preceded them. The new terminus at Blaenau Ffestiniog was eventually built on the former GWR station site and not as shown. The CEA had become the Central Electricity Generating Board. (M.Seymour)

80. The Deviation was begun in January 1965 and Dduallt station was reopened, albeit without a run-round loop, on 6th April 1968. This is the White Rose Group's special train on 26th May 1968, six days after the loop was completed. (J.H.Meredith)

81.    The top end of the loop is seen on the same day with the Simplex near the point where the new track joined the old route. The new embankment for the first part of the spiral is on the right. Some of the original side-tipping Hudson wagon bodies had been turned to create end tippers. They had worked near Chichester where Hants & Sussex Group members had renovated them. (J.H.Meredith)

82.    This picture from 9th February 1969 shows the cast concrete columns designed to take the new route over the old, thus forming Britain's first spiral railway route. They had been completed in the previous month, before the weather worsened. (A.G.W.Garraway)

83.     The finished Rhoslyn Bridge was recorded in June 1971, as *Blanche* nears the end of her journey. A works train is on the new embankment, which did not receive permanent track until more than two years later. (A.G.W.Garraway)

84.     A special train crept as far as Rhoslyn Bridge on 18th July 1971, carrying representatives of John Players who had sponsored the construction of the footbridge at Tan-y-Bwlch. A double engine is entering the station. The first signals appeared here in August 1972. (A.G.W.Garraway)

85. The top end points were removed in November 1988 to leave a siding for the engineers. This itself was provided with a short loop in 1989. Seen from the platform on 26th June 1994 is *Prince* with a terminating goods train during the 1920s Weekend. (J.Scrace)

86. A termporary signal box was erected near the top points in 1977 and its 13-lever frame remained in use until July 1988, when the signal arms for the loop were removed. The posts remained in place until October 2001, when one of the upper tubes was caught on film on its journey to the ground. (G.Cole)

# THE DEVIATION ENTERPRISE

87.     Rhoslyn Bridge is in the background of this photo from July 1973, which shows the heavy rail section used for the permanent way. The Wales Tourist Board announced in 1975 that it would make a 49% grant towards the cost of the Deviation, the compensation for the loss of the original route falling far short of it. This was known as "Barn" site. The temporary platform was for a special train run on 7th July 1973. (A.G.W.Garraway)

88.    Map III shows the 1836 reservoir and dam which were created to provide power for one of the inclines. Work started on 16th October 1971 to make a gap in the dam for the new route. We see temporary way in place in mid-1974; the sub-soil here was particularly boggy. During that year 6166 loaded skips were moved by hand and 2880 volunteer man days were worked. (A.G.W.Garraway)

89.    This panorama below the tunnel in August 1974 includes the old and new routes, the lower one being retained to serve the mess erected at the site seen in picture 78. A new breed of volunteer was recruited for this massive manual task, helped only by occasional explosive blasts. A Smalley excavator arrived in August 1973. Diesels such as these were of no value on the work sites: *Jane* is below and *Diana* is at the top. (A.G.W.Garraway)

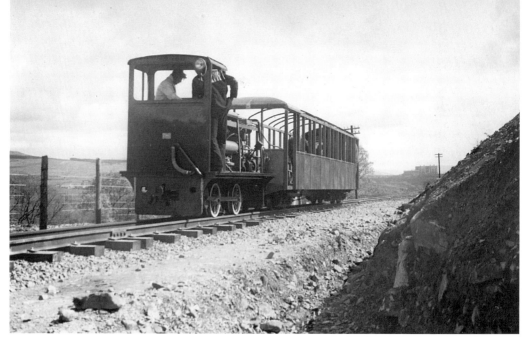

90.      Passengers arriving at Dduallt from 26th May 1975 were offered a trip over part of the new line. This was the first example of push-pull working on the FR and was operated by *Moel Hebog* with coach no. 110. Seen on trial a few weeks earlier, the coach ran unglazed that year, but with a roof. The now-closed Trawsfynydd Nuclear Power Station is in the background. (A.G.W.Garraway)

91.      Work started on the new tunnel on 1st September 1975 and three former tin miners from Cornwall broke through on 1st May 1976. Subsequently it had to be opened out and then lined by shotcreting, an unexpected and tedious task. This is the south end in July 1975. (A.G.W.Garraway)

92.  The same tunnel mouth is in the background of this view of the stone screening equipment in November 1975. The spoil from the tunnel came out on a line behind the sheds and was tipped at the foot of the elevator. It was discharged at the top onto a vibrating screen and dust was shot to the left, track ballast dropped into wagons on the middle line and rocks ran into those on the right. (A.G.W.Garraway)

93.  This is Tunnel North on 28th May 1980 as *Merddin Emrys* passes with the 15.50 from Porthmadog. The tunnel tracklaying was completed in February 1977, but considerable enterprise and tenacity was required to complete it to the satisfaction of the highly demanding authorities. (J.Scrace)

# LLYN YSTRADAU

*(top left)* 94.    Like Dduallt, this area was part of the Deviation, but is being given a separate section. Tunnel North cutting is on the right, beyond the breach in the dam. The roadway to the left of it is on the site of the north incline (1836-42). The mouth of the old tunnel had been near the black triangle, on the left. Also shown is *Upnor Castle* working the 16.30 Porthmadog to Tanygrisiau on 27th August 1979. (J.Scrace)

*(lower left)* 95.    The 17.13 departure from Tanygrisiau was recorded on the same day from the same location, the locomotive being *Merddin Emrys*. Now known as Tanygrisiau Reservoir, Llyn Ystradau gave its name to a station that was situated in the background for the 1977 season. The power station for this pumped storage scheme is above the rear coach and the top of the dam is represented by a white line beyond the water. (J.Scrace)

96.    Beyond and behind the power station a level crossing was needed over the road to the penstocks. The FR was required to build a bridge over the high pressure water pipes to the generators, but it is now hidden underground. Above *Merddin Emrys* and its train in this 1978 view is evidence of the formation of the Wrysgan Quarry incline. (A.G.W.Garraway)

97.    A photograph from March 1963 illustrates the unexpected problems that can arise on the FR. The location is above the station, where the track is on a ledge, but a far greater fall occurred below the line in November 1975. Rocks entered a cottage and remedial work proved very expensive. Such wagons were used by locals as necessary and by your author for his rucksack on a survey in 1951. (A.G.W.Garraway)

98.     The village centre is included in another view above the station, as is the new Dolrhedyn bridge. This was provided by the County Council, who had removed the previous one some years earlier. Its replacement at a higher level than the original presented few problems to the track layers in April 1981; there were liberal helpings of FR enterprise available. (A.G.W.Garraway)

99.    The end of the platform is in sight as the 2-6-2T *Mountaineer* departs for Blaenau Ffestiniog on 22nd July 1991 and regains the original alignment; the close proximity of the boundaries confirm this. At a lower level on the left is the original goods shed. The loop had been lifted in May 1984, but its reinstatement began in 1990. (J.Scrace)

100.    A second new level crossing had to be provided below the station, this being on the road to Llyn Stwlan, the upper lake. *Merddin Emrys* has just passed over it on 3rd May 1993 with the 14.00 from the upper terminus. Coaches 11 and 12 are leading, these having served almost continuously since the reopening. (J.Scrace)

101.    Entering the platform with an up train on the same day is *Prince* piloted by *Upnor Castle*. This powerful machine had been built by F.C.Hibberd in 1954 for the Navy and was regauged from 2ft 6ins for use on the FR in 1968. The rear of this train (also the one in the previous picture) is on the bridge over the River Cwmorthin. Its 55ft long concrete beams were put in place in 1976. (J.Scrace)

102. A tasteful waiting shelter was erected in 1996 and is seen on 31st August 1998 as *David Lloyd George* arrives. Signal posts were erected at both ends of the station in 1997 and most of the loop was laid in 1998. The siding was intended as a refuge for works trains. (V.Mitchell)

103. The construction of a signal box and the provision of signalling, with its associated extensive cabling, occupied a group of volunteers for over ten years. They fitted one arm briefly on 10th September 2000. Fresh management in 2000 decided to abandon all that work in favour of unworked trailing points. This modern system requires no signalman. Some of the team decided to design a solar powered arangement for the indicator lights. (G.Cole)

104.    It seems that clearance of one flangeway was deemed sufficient for the Simplex to cross the Tanygrisiau Road on 5th March 1955, the first time that the gates had been opened since 1946. The adjacent rails were eventually removed, but both tracks were kept in the road until relaying. A disused locomotive shed stood to the right of this view until 1976, when it became part of a new civil engineering depot. (A.G.W.Garraway)

105.    The main building of the depot has a white roof in this photograph from 2nd May 2000. On the left is a spacious carriage shed which was completed in 1997. Its tracks lead to a long headshunt, which runs parallel to the line to Llandudno Junction. (V.Mitchell)

# BLAENAU FFESTINIOG

106.    Two photographs from 3rd July 1950 show the provisions made by the LNWR in 1879-81. The FR added the platform and shelter on the left in 1881. The building in the centre was destroyed by fire and a new one built in 1956. In the goods yard is "Cauliflower" 0-6-0 no. 58365, but it is obscuring the view of the exchange sidings. (J.H.Meredith)

107.    The slate traffic to the exchange sidings from the Maenofferen Quarry was hauled by the diesel seen here. It ran over that part of the FR that did not close in 1946 and also northwards to the Oakeley Quarry. The former section carried its last slate on 3rd November 1962. (J.H.Meredith)

108. The incline to the Maenofferen Quarry began at the end of the FR at Duffws, where the passenger station was in use until 1930. It now serves as the public toilets at the car park. The quarry was one of the few still to be working at the beginning of the 21st century. This photograph is from July 1951, when the lease of the track was supplementing cottage rents to keep the FR afloat. (A.G.W.Garraway)

109. Manager Garraway is at the controls of the Simplex (named *Mary Ann* in 1963) as it enters "Steison Fein" (narrow station - seen in picture 106) on 5th February 1955, the first movement since 1946. The booking office sign still showed the fares, just. (A.G.W.Garraway)

110. Exactly one month later the Simplex was recorded at the platform that had served the GWR station until September 1939. In the background is Queens Bridge under which the line passed to Duffws station. Maenofferen Quarry's diesel locomotive was kept in a compound under this bridge, which carried Church Street. The structure was demolished in 1980, the former GWR station having closed to passengers in 1960 and to goods in 1961. (A.G.W.Garraway)

111.    This July 1980 view towards the former LNWR station features the line that was opened on 26th April 1964 to link it with the former GWR route, which was used for the conveyance of nuclear waste flasks. The road bridge had been built in 1963, its right span being intended for the traffic mentioned in caption 107. The left one of the two concrete tubes would take FR trains from 1982. (A.G.W.Garraway)

**Blaenau,** 72/12/10,60-1, Station site discussed at joint Society-Company Board Meeting.

Five sites considered; a) the former FR/GWR (Central) station (wrong side of several bridges); b) the former GWR slate yard [as (a) but site earmarked for school]; c) the former LNWR station, to be a joint BR/FR station (gradient too steep); d) 'Stesion Fein' (narrow station), the old FR Exchange station, opposite the BR site; line could curve south for extra space; and

e) Glan-y-pwll; choice of the meeting, cheap, easy, with simple connection to Dinas branch, declared the only possible first terminus', with an option on Stesion Fein for later expansion.

112.   The GWR station site was cleared, apart from the Trawsfynydd track, in preparation for a joint BR/FR terminus estimated to cost £0.34m. The funds came from several different sources, including Brussels. The footings seen in this August 1980 view were for the wall shown in the next picture. The lower rear rooms in "The Queens" (left of centre) accommodated the FR booking office and shop from 1997. (A.G.W.Garraway)

**Blaenau,** 81/11/20,95-9, The Conversion of Glan-y-pwll house into two separate flats has now been completed. Work on the roofless Glan-y-pwll depot building completed by mid-October and roofing contractors had arrived. mid-November.

**Blaenau,** 81/11/20,95-12, Various footbridges progressing. Old water tank plinth at Exchange demolished. Light Railway Order sought to replace gates with lights at Glan-y-pwll. Ballast laid from Central almost to Glan-y-pwll crossing. Permanent track almost up to crossing to be continued across into Central during January.

113.  The bunting was out for the opening of the BR platform on 22nd March 1982. A special train stands on the loop line and in front of it can be seen the head of steel of the FR. There was little more track to add and train operation began eight weeks later, amidst great celebration. For years the timetable had stated "Service temporarily suspended" and at last the enterprise of so many had created a complete railway.  (A.G.W.Garraway)

114.    There was still much to be done and this house above the station had to accommodate the booking office for 15 years. "Isallt" was also used for the Tourist Information Centre and was thus severely overcrowded at times.  (A.G.W.Garraway)

115.    A panorama from 30th July 1983 has "Isallt" top right, an S shape path leading down to the BR platform and the right-angled footbridge to the FR one. This has temporary huts on it for tickets and toilets. Curving away from the water tank (left of centre) is the trackbed of the line that once served Newborough Mills, where writing slates were produced for children at schools unable to afford much paper. (A.G.W.Garraway)

116.    The 13.45 departure on 27th May 1985 was hauled by *Earl of Merioneth* which was completed at Boston Lodge in 1979. Hunslet made the boiler and existing power bogies were used. The large tanks gave good water and oil capacity. Oil firing had been introduced on the FR as a means of preventing destruction of the environment by fire, due to sparks. No. 47480 is waiting to depart for Llandudno. (J.Scrace)

117.    *Mountaineer* is behind *Merddin Emrys* on the 17.00 departure on 6th May 1990; the platform canopy had been completed earlier that year. The second water outlet had been provided for the day when that platform might be used. An early idea was that a shuttle service could be run to the foot of the incline to Llechwedd Quarrry. (J.Scrace)

118.    At "The Hunslet 100 Grand Steam Gala", ex-PQR sisters *Blanche* and *Linda* run round their train on 3rd May 1993. The latter had been adapted by an enterprising works manager in 1985 to the spark-free producer gas system, whereby coal is heated in the firebox to produce gas which is burnt. DMU no. 101685 waits alongside no. 37422, which is standing with the empty stock of the 08.35 from Crewe. It was named *Robert F.Fairlie Locomotive Engineer 1831-1885*. (J.Scrace)

119. *David Lloyd George* was recorded taking water on 1st May 1999, by which time the second outlet had been removed. However, track had been laid at the second platform in 1997 to allow two trains to terminate here. The block under the footbridge is at the end of a short siding added soon afterwards to accommodate locomotives running round. The associated new signals were still covered. (V.Mitchell)

120. A service train and an empty one were combined on 4th May 2001 and one of the empty cars derailed upon entering platform 2. It displaced the lever frame, which luckily was redundant due to the provision of point motors. All coaches, except no. 105, were back in service the next day. (Ian Ward)

121. Following withdrawal of nuclear waste trains, a foot crossing was completed in October 1998, this giving direct access to the car park. The ugly ramp for the footbridge was replaced by steps. No. 153356 stands by the stop board, the "Heritage" DMUs having been finally displaced in May 2000. (V.Mitchell)

# FOOTNOTE

In a volume of this size covering 50 years, it has been possible to illustrate only selected examples of the diverse enterprises that have formed part of the resuscitation process.

Each location on the route deserves a book of its own to illustrate its evolution from dereliction to full vitalilty and the rich variety of characters that have brought it about.

Few of the people appearing in the photographs herein have been identified. Maybe a proposal considered by members of the Heritage Group to name those who have appeared in all books on the FR will come to fruition before it is too late.

I hope that this publication will have given an insight to those with a limited knowledge of this historic line into some of the events and changes that have made it a world leader again.

Details of FRS membership and of groups are always available from Harbour Station.

# THE TRAVEL ENTERPRISE

Alan Heywood, Managing Director

The origins of Ffestiniog Travel can be found in the Beeching era when almost all Cambrian Coast line stations were fully staffed. The route was a prime candidate for rationalisation which included the destaffing of some stations and fare collection at these places put in the hands of train guards. Two things need to be remembered here. Firstly, "pay trains" were very uncommon at that time. Secondly, the Cambrian had been threatened with closure many times and the public and local media were deeply suspicious of any move which could be construed as closure by stealth.

In an unusual move, BR approached the FR to seek its views on taking over the ticket issuing at Minffordd, where staffing ceased on 19th October 1964. This was agreed, although Minffordd was subsequently only ever manned when the FR had staff on duty for train crossing purposes and, in practice, most tickets were issued at Porthmadog right from the outset.

Not long afterwards, Portmadoc (FR) found itself in the position of becoming the "clearing house" for all kinds of BR matters including lost property and complaints! In this respect, the FR was never seen by the local people as a travel agency. Harbour Station was a "real" railway station which sold tickets to either Tan-y-Bwlch (in those days) or London! This subtlety was important - the FR had hitherto been regarded by some local inhabitants as a place for mad Englishmen to play trains. Now it performed a service to the community in much the same way as did the post office or the bank!

The next stage in the story came in 1973. Mair Watson, then senior booking clerk in Porthmadog, noticed that a number of overseas visitors came to North Wales without tickets for their return. She was able to help as far as the English coast but no further and so the FR applied for a licence to sell Sealink and continental rail tickets. This time, instead of BR begging the FR for help, it was the other way round and BR was deeply suspicious of the FR's ability to generate sufficient business in a rural area to justify the costs to BR of maintaining an agency. A target was set for the first year's trading, staff were sent on residential courses to learn continental timetabling and ticketing.

There remained the question of how to meet the target set by BR. Their real interest was earning money for the Sealink routes and so the easiest way was to find the longest route (Harwich to Hook of Holland) and then for a group to use it. Groups who wish to holiday at the Hook of Holland are not easy to find but why not arrange a holiday to the Swiss narrow gauge lines for FR supporters and others and sell it? Of course hotels would be required and the tour would need to include the very best Alpine scenery to make it attractive but, why not? And so, in October 1974, what was then intended as a one-off tour to the Swiss Alps set out. Ffestiniog Travel was born.

This tour was so well subscribed (68 customers) that, within Switzerland, it was divided into clockwise and anticlockwise groups and, inevitably, a market was perceived for future tours and destinations.

Scandinavia followed in April 1975 and there was another tour to Switzerland in September. Nevertheless, travel was very much a spare time activity for booking office staff throughout the 1970s and only 412 customers were taken abroad in the whole of the first six years of operation.

An important milestone was passed in 1979 when the first long haul tour (to Canada) was run. Another followed in 1980 but, when Canada drastically reduced its rail services at very short notice in 1981, no further attempts were made to go long haul until 1985, when a very successful tour to Japan was run. By 1987 the situation in Canada was stable once more and three tours were operated that year followed by the first to the USA in 1988.

Meanwhile a new and very significant niche was beginning to open up. In 1981, a small number of customers approached the company for tailor made arrangements. Nowadays, such customers, together with private groups, account for almost two thirds of the total business.

Ffestiniog Travel was an integral part of the Commercial Department of the Ffestiniog Railway until 1992, when the decision was taken to split it out as a separate company. Profits from the Travel operation would continue to be used solely to benefit the FR by being covenanted to the FR Trust, then finding their way back to the FR in the form of capital grants. Much of the refurbishment of the ex-Lynton and Barnstaple Railway buffet car and the new ladies toilets at Harbour Station were financed in this way, not to mention the total cost of brand new coach no. 122 finished in 2002. A total of £250,812 passed via this route between 1993 and 2000.

Nowadays Ffestiniog Travel undertakes a lot of contract work for other organisations, especially educational establishments, where the customer supplies the tour leader/tutor; we provide the transport and accommodation. As the graph shows, we arrange many tours and will gladly send you our comprehensive brochure. You can support the FR by asking us to supply all your rail tickets, also those of all your friends and relations! Whether its for your next trip to London or a single to Vladivostock, a telephone call should result in the ticket being on your doormat within a day or two.

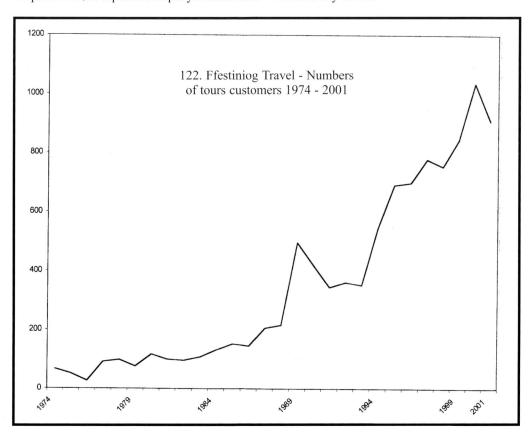

122. Ffestiniog Travel - Numbers of tours customers 1974 - 2001

# MP Middleton Press

Easebourne Lane, Midhurst, W Sussex. GU29 9AZ Tel: 01730 813169 Fax: 01730 812601
*If books are not available from your local transport stockist, order direct with cheque,*
*Visa or Mastercard, post free UK.*

## BRANCH LINES
Branch Line to Allhallows
Branch Line to Alton
Branch Lines around Ascot
Branch Line to Ashburton
Branch Lines around Bodmin
Branch Line to Bude
Branch Lines around Canterbury
Branch Lines around Chard & Yeovil
Branch Line to Cheddar
Branch Lines around Cromer
Branch Lines to East Grinstead
Branch Lines of East London
Branch Lines to Effingham Junction
Branch Lines around Exmouth
Branch Lines to Falmouth, Helston & St. Ives
Branch Line to Fairford
Branch Lines around Gosport
Branch Line to Hayling
Branch Lines to Henley, Windsor & Marlow
Branch Line to Hawkhurst
Branch Lines around Huntingdon
Branch Line to Ilfracombe
Branch Line to Kingswear
Branch Line to Lambourn
Branch Lines to Launceston & Princetown
Branch Line to Looe
Branch Line to Lyme Regis
Branch Lines around Midhurst
Branch Line to Minehead
Branch Line to Moretonhampstead
Branch Lines to Newport
Branch Lines to Newquay
Branch Lines around North Woolwich
Branch Line to Padstow
Branch Lines around Plymouth
Branch Lines to Seaton and Sidmouth
Branch Line to Selsey
Branch Lines around Sheerness
Branch Line to Shrewsbury
Branch Line to Swanage *updated*
Branch Line to Tenterden
Branch Lines around Tiverton
Branch Lines to Torrington
Branch Line to Upwell
Branch Lines of West London
Branch Lines around Weymouth
Branch Lines around Wimborne
Branch Lines around Wisbech

## NARROW GAUGE
Branch Line to Lynton
Branch Lines around Portmadoc 1923-46
Branch Lines around Porthmadog 1954-94
Branch Line to Southwold
Douglas to Port Erin
Kent Narrow Gauge
Northern France Narrow Gauge
Romneyrail
Southern France Narrow Gauge
Sussex Narrow Gauge
Two-Foot Gauge Survivors
Vivarais Narrow Gauge

## SOUTH COAST RAILWAYS
Ashford to Dover
Bournemouth to Weymouth
Brighton to Worthing
Eastbourne to Hastings
Hastings to Ashford
Portsmouth to Southampton
Ryde to Ventnor
Southampton to Bournemouth

## SOUTHERN MAIN LINES
Basingstoke to Salisbury
Bromley South to Rochester
Crawley to Littlehampton
Dartford to Sittingbourne
East Croydon to Three Bridges
Epsom to Horsham
Exeter to Barnstaple
Exeter to Tavistock
Faversham to Dover
London Bridge to East Croydon
Orpington to Tonbridge
Tonbridge to Hastings
Salisbury to Yeovil
Sittingbourne to Ramsgate
Swanley to Ashford
Tavistock to Plymouth
Three Bridges to Brighton
Victoria to Bromley South
Victoria to East Croydon
Waterloo to Windsor
Waterloo to Woking
Woking to Portsmouth
Woking to Southampton
Yeovil to Exeter

## EASTERN MAIN LINES
Barking to Southend
Ely to Kings Lynn
Fenchurch Street to Barking
Ipswich to Saxmundham
Liverpool Street to Ilford
Saxmundham to Yarmouth

## WESTERN MAIN LINES
Ealing to Slough
Exeter to Newton Abbot
Newton Abbot to Plymouth
Newbury to Westbury
Paddington to Ealing
Paddington to Princes Risborough
Plymouth to St. Austell
Reading to Didcot
Slough to Newbury
St. Austell to Penzance
Taunton to Exeter
Westbury to Taunton

## MIDLAND MAIN LINES
St. Pancras to St. Albans

## COUNTRY RAILWAY ROUTES
Andover to Southampton
Bath to Evercreech Junction
Bournemouth to Evercreech Junction
Burnham to Evercreech Junction
Cheltenham to Andover
Croydon to East Grinstead
Didcot to Winchester
East Kent Light Railway
Fareham to Salisbury
Guildford to Redhill
Reading to Basingstoke
Reading to Guildford
Redhill to Ashford
Salisbury to Westbury
Stratford upon Avon to Cheltenham
Strood to Paddock Wood
Taunton to Barnstaple
Wenford Bridge to Fowey
Westbury to Bath
Woking to Alton
Yeovil to Dorchester

## GREAT RAILWAY ERAS
Ashford from Steam to Eurostar
Clapham Junction 50 years of change
Festiniog in the Fifties
Festiniog in the Sixties
Festiniog 50 years of enterprise
Isle of Wight Lines 50 years of change
Railways to Victory 1944-46
Return to Blaenau 1970-82
SECR Centenary album
Talyllyn 50 years of change
Yeovil 50 years of change

## LONDON SUBURBAN RAILWAYS
Caterham and Tattenham Corner
Charing Cross to Dartford
Clapham Jn. to Beckenham Jn.
Crystal Palace (HL) & Catford Loop
East London Line
Finsbury Park to Alexandra Palace
Holbourn Viaduct to Lewisham
Kingston and Hounslow Loops
Lewisham to Dartford
Lines around Wimbledon
London Bridge to Addiscombe
Mitcham Junction Lines
North London Line
South London Line
West Croydon to Epsom
West London Line
Willesden Junction to Richmond
Wimbledon to Beckenham
Wimbledon to Epsom

## STEAMING THROUGH
Steaming through Cornwall
Steaming through the Isle of Wight
Steaming through Kent
Steaming through West Hants
Steaming through West Sussex

## TRAMWAY CLASSICS
Aldgate & Stepney Tramways
Barnet & Finchley Tramways
Bath Tramways
Brighton's Tramways
Bristol's Tramways
Burton & Ashby Tramways
Camberwell & W.Norwood Tramways
Clapham & Streatham Tramways
Croydon's Tramways
Dover's Tramways
East Ham & West Ham Tramways
Edgware and Willesden Tramways
Eltham & Woolwich Tramways
Embankment & Waterloo Tramways
Enfield & Wood Green Tramways
Exeter & Taunton Tramways
Greenwich & Dartford Tramways
Hammersmith & Hounslow Tramways
Hampstead & Highgate Tramways
Hastings Tramways
Holborn & Finsbury Tramways
Ilford & Barking Tramways
Kingston & Wimbledon Tramways
Lewisham & Catford Tramways
Liverpool Tramways 1. Eastern Routes
Liverpool Tramways 2. Southern Routes
Liverpool Tramways 3. Northern Routes
Maidstone & Chatham Tramways
Margate to Ramsgate
North Kent Tramways
Norwich Tramways
Reading Tramways
Seaton & Eastbourne Tramways
Shepherds Bush & Uxbridge Tramways
Southend-on-sea Tramways
Southwark & Deptford Tramways
Stamford Hill Tramways
Twickenham & Kingston Tramways
Victoria & Lambeth Tramways
Waltham Cross & Edmonton Tramways
Walthamstow & Leyton Tramways
Wandsworth & Battersea Tramways

## TROLLEYBUS CLASSICS
Bournemouth Trolleybuses
Croydon Trolleybuses
Derby Trolleybuses
Hastings Trolleybuses
Maidstone Trolleybuses
Portsmouth Trolleybuses
Woolwich & Dartford Trolleybuses

## WATERWAY ALBUMS
Kent and East Sussex Waterways
London to Portsmouth Waterway
West Sussex Waterways

## MILITARY BOOKS
Battle over Portsmouth
Battle over Sussex 1940
Bombers over Sussex 1943-45
Bognor at War
Military Defence of West Sussex
Military Signals from the South Coast
Secret Sussex Resistance
Surrey Home Guard

## OTHER RAILWAY BOOKS
Index to all Middleton Press stations
Industrial Railways of the South-East
South Eastern & Chatham Railways
London Chatham & Dover Railway
War on the Line (SR 1939-45)

## BIOGRAPHY
Garraway Father & Son